What Did Jesus Do?

MARY MANZ SIMON

ILLUSTRATED BY ANNE KENNEDY

Thomas Nelson, Inc.

Nashville

For Christina Marie Simon, Matthew 6:33–34
—Mary Manz Simon

For Mom, a "big soul,"
from Annie, a "little soul"

Text copyright © 1998 by Mary Manz Simon
Illustrations © 1998 by Anne Kennedy

Published in Nashville, Tennessee, by Tommy Nelson™, a division of Thomas Nelson, Inc. Managing Editor: Laura Minchew; Editor: Tama Fortner

Scripture quotations are from The Holy Bible, New Century Version, copyright © 1987, 1988, 1991 by Word Publishing, Nashville, Tennessee. Used by permission.

Library of Congress Cataloging-in-Publication Data

Simon, Mary Manz, 1948–
    What did Jesus do? / by Mary Manz Simon ; illustrated by Anne Kennedy.
      p. cm.
    Contents: Obedience—Friendship—Honesty—Forgiveness—Kindness—Trust—Humility—Thankfulness.
    ISBN 0-8499-5855-5
    1. Virtues—Juvenile literature. 2. Bible stories, English—N.T. Gospels. 3. Jesus Christ—Example—Juvenile literature. [1. Bible stories—N.T. 2. Virtues. 3. Conduct of life.] I. Kennedy, Anne, 1955– ill. II. Title.
    BV4630.S55   1998
    241'.4—dc21   98-22529
                                                           CIP
                                                           AC

Printed in the United States of America

98 99 00 01 02 03 LBM 9 8 7 6 5 4 3 2 1

To the Adult

As an educator and mother of three, I care deeply about helping children develop a set of core values.

Many adults and older children embrace the "What would Jesus do?" concept. But developmentally, because young children cannot mentally change places with someone else, they can't think how someone else would respond in a specific instance. As a result, the WWJD phenomenon has had minimal impact on younger children.

However, young children copy and personally internalize behaviors modeled for them. That's why the book you hold in your hands illustrates what Jesus actually did in situations similar to those that children face every day. By looking at what Jesus did, even young children can learn to look to Him for answers to problems today.

Dr. Mary Manz Simon

Contents

Playing by the Rules

A Story about Obedience

Cole leaned over to look at the clock. Only 4:26? It felt like he'd been practicing more than 11 minutes.

"Hey, Cole, done yet?" a voice drifted in through the open window.

Grateful for an excuse to leave the piano, Cole scooted off the bench. "I've got to practice until 4:45," he answered.

"But your mom isn't home," Jason said. "She'll never know."

Cole looked at the clock again. 4:28. The house rule was clear: Practicing piano came before playing with friends. Making up his mind to break the rule, he grabbed his glove and cap.

Cole sailed out the back door.

"You practiced fast today," Kate said, flipping the ball into the air.

9

Half an hour later, a familiar voice called, "Hey, team."

"Hi, Mom," Cole answered, without taking his eyes off the ball.

"Sorry, kids, but the ballpark is closing for today," said his mom.

"See ya," Cole yelled to his friends. He swung on the gate to close it, then went inside for a drink.

"Cole, Mrs. Palmer must have phoned while you were outside," his mom said. "I saved the message for you."

"Thanks," he said between large slurps.

10

The smooth voice of Mrs. Palmer drifted into the room.

"You've practiced so faithfully, Cole, that I've chosen you to open next week's recital," the recorded voice played back. "Congratulations!"

Cole's shoulders slumped.

"Practiced so faithfully . . ." he groaned. The phrase bounced around in his head all evening. What was that story in the Bible about obedience?

"I'm going fishing," Peter announced.

John, Thomas, and some of Jesus' other disciples climbed into the boat after Peter. It seemed like a good night for fishing. Again and again, the men threw out their nets. Again and again, they hauled them back empty. The disciples fished all night, but they didn't catch a single fish.

Early the next morning, a man waved to them from the shore. The man shouted, "Catch anything?"

The fishermen yelled back, "No!"

Then the man called, "Drop your nets on the right side of the boat, and you'll find some fish."

Peter grumbled, "Here we work all night and don't catch a thing, then some wise guy thinks we'll find fish on the other side of the boat."

Thomas and John untangled the nets. The men balanced themselves carefully as they threw out the huge nets on the right side of the boat.

Immediately, fish started flopping in the nets. The nets became so full that some fish flipped back out and swam away.

John looked at the loaded nets and said, "The man we obeyed is Jesus."

Peter jumped out of the boat and swam toward the shore. The other disciples guided the boat back to land, dragging the heavy nets behind them.

Jesus had already started a fire on the beach.

"Bring some of the fish you caught," Jesus directed.

This time, Peter obeyed Jesus without grumbling. He dragged one of the nets onto the beach.

One hundred fifty-three very large fish
were flopping in the nets.
Jesus invited, "Come and eat breakfast."
The disciples obeyed again. They wanted
to follow Jesus in every way.

After school the next day, Cole settled at the piano as his friends' voices floated in from outside.

"Hey, Keyboard Cole," Jason yelled through the window. "Aren't you coming?"

"I'll be out at 4:45," Cole said and banged the window shut.

18

Knock. Knock. Knock. Jason came to the door.

"Your mom will *never* know if you practice inside or play outside," Jason said.

"But *I* will," Cole explained. "If I don't follow the rules, I *feel* bad."

"Leave him alone, Jason," Amanda said. "Cole's doing the right thing."

"Gotcha," said Kate, sneaking up to snatch Jason's cap.

"Hey," yelled Jason, turning to chase after her.

"I'll be out soon," Cole said with a smile. "At 4:45."

Children, obey your parents as the Lord wants, because this is the right thing to do.
—Ephesians 6:1 NCV

Flying Lunches

A Story about Friendship

It was almost noon when the five students puffed up the hill to the zoo picnic area.

"I'm starved," Jason announced, as he began rummaging through the lunch bags.

"Jason," called Mrs. Meyer, "since you're already into the lunches, you can hand out the bags."

"I'm really just looking for mine," Jason muttered. He had had an awful morning. T. J., the new student, was not only smart, but *everyone* accepted him as if they had all been friends forever.

Jason angrily tossed the bags to
his classmates.

"Here's the new kid's bag," snapped Jason,
as the bag sailed high in the air.

T. J. jumped, but the bag flew beyond his outstretched
hand. Dismayed, he ran to see where his lunch had gone.

"Squawk, squawk, squawk."

A flurry of feathers pointed to the landing site. Ducks
and geese waddled over to inspect the foreign objects.

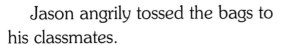

"Now look what you've done," Amanda scolded as she turned to face Jason. "What's T. J. going to eat?"

"Come on," Cole said. "I'll share."

"I'll share, too," said Amanda.

T. J. smiled his thanks while Cole marched over to Jason, who was busy munching.

"What are *you* sharing?" Cole demanded.

"Huh?" Jason asked, getting ready to take a big bite of his sandwich.

"What are *you* giving T. J.?" Cole repeated. "Remember the story we heard at church about friends?"

"Oh, yeah," Jason mumbled, chewing as he remembered. "The roof guys."

"Whoops!" Eli was so excited, he almost tripped over his own feet. He was in a hurry to tell his friend the big news.

"Jonas, Jesus is in town!" Eli called out.

Jonas looked up through tired eyes.

"Jesus is in town," Eli repeated. "Jesus can heal you!"

"I can't get to where Jesus is," Jonas said, smiling weakly. Jonas had been unable to walk for a very long time. If only Jesus could heal him!

"We will carry you," Eli said firmly. "We'll pick up your bed and take you to Jesus." Then Eli raced to get his friends.

When Eli returned, the four men carefully carried Jonas to the house where Jesus was teaching.

The crowd was so large, it overflowed out the door. The men could not even hear Jesus speak.

"This will not work," Jonas observed. "Thank you, my friends, but I can't even crawl through that crowd."

Then Eli had an idea. Scrambling up to the roof, he signaled his friends from the top.

"We can take off part of the roof," Eli said. "Then we can lower Jonas down to Jesus."

Carefully, the four friends carried Jonas on his bed up the stairs. Panting and sweating, they finally reached the roof. Cautiously, Eli started removing pieces of the roof.

"Whoops!" Eli said with a friendly wave, as dirt floated down on the richly dressed men below.

At last, the opening was large enough for the bed.

Slowly the four men lowered Jonas into the room below. Shouts and laughter floated up as the crowd watched Jonas enter through the roof.

Jesus smiled up at the men who were such good friends to Jonas. Then Jesus healed Jonas. Eli was so excited, he almost fell through the hole in the roof.

"Jonas, Jesus healed you!" The men rejoiced with their friend.

"Yes," cried Jonas. "But I wouldn't even be here if it weren't for my friends. I am grateful to Jesus and thankful for you."

Jason got up from the picnic table. Walking toward the group, he slid a small bag of cookies across the table to T. J.

"I'm full," Jason said.

"Thanks, Jason," T. J. said, shoving the cookies back across the table. "But I'm full, too. My friends gave me a big lunch."

Jason looked down at the cookies.

". . . wanted to share," he mumbled.

"Well, then, these will be a great snack for the trip home," said
T. J. He examined the bag, then looked up with a broad smile. "I
counted. There are just enough for each of us to have one."

"All set group?" Cole asked.
"Lead on!" T. J. answered for everyone.

A friend loves you all the time.
—Proverbs 17:17 NCV

The Race

A Story about Forgiveness

"Your new bike is beautiful, Cole," said Amanda. She had always wanted a bike like Cole's.

"Ready to race?" asked Jason.

"Amanda and I can't race against Cole's new bike," said Kate.

"Aw, come on," said Jason.

Kate shrugged her shoulders. With a reluctant "Okay," she and Amanda pedaled to the usual starting line. Jason gave the countdown, and the trio whizzed off. Right at the start, Cole zoomed ahead.

"You were right," Amanda called to Kate. "We can't win against Cole anymore!"

As they reached the finish line, Amanda skidded in a cloud of gravel and dust. Her tire hit a rock, and she careened into Cole's bike. Tumbling onto the gravel path, Amanda and both bikes fell in a jumbled heap.

"Are you all right?" Kate asked cautiously.

"I think so," Amanda said slowly. Turning around, she saw Cole kneeling by his new bike. The front wheel cover had smashed into the tire.

"Oh, Cole, I'm so sorry!" said Amanda.

"That's okay," he said softly. "At least you weren't hurt."

The group looked silently at the bent metal.

"I'll help you carry the bike home so the tire won't get cut," Jason offered.

"Thanks," Cole said, then added, "Amanda, I'm really glad you didn't get hurt."

"Thanks," Amanda said.

Later, at Kate's house, Amanda waited for her dad to pick her up.

"I'm really sorry I messed up Cole's bike," Amanda said.

"But he forgave you," Kate reminded her. "'Forgive' means 'forget,' remember?"

Amanda smiled, remembering the last time she had heard the word, 'forgive.'

Jesus told this story about a man with two sons.

"Dad," the younger son said to his father. "I don't want to stay here and work. I want my share of the family's money now. I want to have fun."

Soon the boy left home with his treasure.

He threw big parties. He spent money everywhere. He wore rich clothes. He ate fabulous meals. He made friends with famous people.

He had a terrific time until he ran out of money. Then, his new friends left. He sold everything, but he still didn't have enough money to live.

His clothes wore out. His sandals fell apart. And his stomach growled all the time. He finally got a job feeding pigs.

"Here piggy, piggy," he called. He was so hungry, even the pigs' food looked good!

As the well-fed pigs rolled in the mud, the young man thought back to his wonderful life at home. He remembered his father and the servants and the good food.

"I will return home," he decided. "I will ask my father to forgive me. I will beg him to hire me as a servant."

As he started home, he thought again and again about asking for forgiveness. Would his father forgive him? Or, would he send him away as he deserved?

When the father saw his son stumbling down the road, he ran out to meet the boy.

The son knelt in the dusty road and said hoarsely, "Father, I have done terrible things. I wasted all the money." The son sobbed. "I made many mistakes. Father, I am so very sorry."

Tears stained the boy's dirty face. His father's heart softened as he accepted his son's apology.

"Everyone, be glad with me!" the father shouted to his servants. "Let's celebrate. My son has come home!"

"Bring him new sandals, new clothes, and an expensive ring. Set a great feast," the father continued.

The son was amazed as people rushed around to serve him. He felt so blessed. He had made terrible mistakes, but his father had forgiven him.

Toot, toot.

Headlights shone through the window. Amanda hurried outside to the familiar car.

"Sorry I'm late, honey," said her dad, reaching to lift her bike into the trunk. "I didn't expect the meeting to last that long."

"No problem," Amanda said tiredly.

"So you forgive me?" her dad asked, reaching to give her a hug.

"Forgive you?" Amanda asked, looking up with surprise.

"Yes, forgive me for being so late," her dad repeated.

"Of course, Dad," Amanda answered with a smile. "I know how good it feels to be forgiven."

Forgive, and you will be forgiven.
—Luke 6:37 NCV

Honest to Goodness

A Story about Honesty

"Whew! I'm hot," Cole said, draining the last few drops from his water bottle.

"With that tournament coming up, Coach is really making us run," Kate said.

"Aw, you're just not in shape," said Jason, as he sauntered by. "I played so well, I'm going to treat myself to some ice cream." Jason nodded toward the frozen delights painted on the delivery truck parked in front of the convenience mart.

Kate, Cole, and Amanda
watched their teammate
stroll toward the store.

"Just looking at that ice cream cools me off," Cole admitted.

"You *must* be hot, if even a picture looks good," Kate said
with a chuckle.

Jason watched his teammates out of the corner of his eye. But
he was *more* interested in the boxes being unloaded off the truck.

The driver jumped into the back of the truck and scratched his head. "Hey, kid," he called down. "You see another box?"

Jason shrugged.

The driver glanced around, then rolled down the back door and jumped to the ground.

"Short a box," he mumbled to himself as he climbed into the cab and slammed the door.

"Hey, guys," Jason called to his teammates. "Look what I found."

Steam rose as he pulled the box out into the sun.

"A breathing box," Amanda giggled.

"The truck driver must have forgotten it," said Cole, glancing suspiciously at Jason.

Jason looked over his shoulder. They were alone in the lot. "Help yourself," he offered.

"That would be stealing," Cole said. "We can't do that. Remember the story in church last week? The one where Jesus talked about honesty."

"I love being rich," Zacchaeus said with a satisfied, if somewhat evil, smile. He was a tax collector, and charging people more taxes than they really owed had made him a wealthy man.

This day began like any other day. But something happened that changed not just the way Zacchaeus collected taxes, but his whole life.

Jesus came to town.

Wherever Jesus went, huge crowds gathered as He healed and taught the people. On this day, Jesus was walking through the city of Jericho when a crowd began to gather near the tax table.

Now Zacchaeus was curious about Jesus. He wanted to see who was pulling people away from his tax table. But there were so many people lining the streets, he couldn't see Jesus.

Zacchaeus tried to stand on a rock, but he slipped off. Zacchaeus tried to climb on a camel, but the camel would not stay still. Then, Zacchaeus saw his answer: a tree. A tree wasn't slippery, and a tree wouldn't move. He scooted up the trunk and eased out on a branch. Now, he could see Jesus.

The crowd beneath Zacchaeus surged forward. People were shouting and calling to Jesus. Zacchaeus slid farther out on the branch so that he had a clear view. Then Jesus stopped right underneath Zacchaeus.

"Come down, Zacchaeus," Jesus said. "I am going to stay at your house today."

Zacchaeus scurried down to welcome Jesus.

The people in the crowd mumbled and complained. Everyone knew about Zacchaeus. They knew he was dishonest. They knew he cheated them. They knew Zacchaeus was a sinner. The murmur in the crowd grew louder.

Then Zacchaeus told Jesus, "I will give half of my money to the poor. And I will pay back four times the amount I have cheated people. Beginning right now, I will be an honest man."

Steam still rose from the box.

"Let's get the box inside before everything melts," Cole said.

"Seems like a waste to me," Jason remarked. "Who'd miss a little ice cream?"

"But it's the right thing to do," Cole insisted. Jason shrugged as his teammates carried the box inside.

Moments later, the trio emerged from the store, smiling broadly.

"The lady at the register gave us these for free," Cole explained. "She didn't even know a box was missing."

"Being honest sure tastes good,"
said Amanda.

An honest witness tells the truth.
—Proverbs 12:17 NCV

The Coonskin Cap

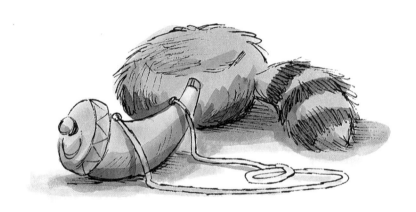

A Story about Kindness

Tears stung T. J.'s eyes. He turned away from the bulletin board. He didn't want his classmates to see his reaction to the play list.

"Hey, T. J., what part did you get?" Cole asked.

"Uh, I don't know," T. J. replied honestly. He had only read one line: Daniel Boone—Jason.

"Don't you want to know?" Cole persisted.

Reluctantly T. J. looked. Since he wasn't going to be Daniel Boone, it really didn't matter.

"Canoe carrier—T. J.," Cole read excitedly, jabbing the page with his finger. "Me too, see?"

T. J. looked, but he still couldn't believe he wasn't going to be Daniel Boone. T. J. had been so excited to find out about the class play at his new school. The coonskin cap he had bought on vacation would be perfect.

"Maybe they'll use a real canoe again this year," Cole said. He was so excited that he didn't notice how miserable T. J. was.

At school during the next few weeks, Jason threw himself into the lead role. Everyone agreed he made a terrific wilderness leader. Costumes were made to fit. And each day, more props were located.

"Coonskin cap," Mrs. Meyer read. "Where can we find a cap for Jason?"

T. J. knew: The coonskin cap was hanging in his closet. But he just sat there. As he sat, he remembered a story about kindness that his dad had read one night for family devotions.

Jesus told this story about kindness.

One day, a man was traveling on a road between two cities. The sun grew warm, and the man stopped to loosen his robe.

Suddenly, robbers jumped out from behind a huge rock. They ripped his clothes, tore away his money pouch, and beat him up. Then they dumped him to die on the dusty road.

The poor traveler could not lift his head to see, but he heard the clop, clop, clop of someone's walking stick.

"Help me," he called weakly as the sound came closer.

A priest leaned on his walking stick, glanced at the injured traveler, and then hurried away.

The traveler lay still in the dusty road. His throat was dry, and his body ached. But he heard the barest swish, swish, swish of the robe worn by church workers.

"Help me," the injured man called weakly.

The church worker hurried past without a second glance.

The aching traveler grew even weaker. He thought he was going to die.

Soon he heard the distant clip clop, clip clop
of a donkey.

Clip clop, clip clop. The sound drew closer.

Then there was silence as the donkey stopped.

"You poor man," said a voice with
a heavy accent. "I must help you."

Carefully, the foreigner washed the traveler's wounds. Then he lifted the traveler onto the donkey. And slowly he led his donkey with the injured man to a nearby inn.

Kindly and gently, he settled the traveler in a room and then paid for his care.

Before the foreigner left the next day, he gave the innkeeper extra money to care for the traveler.

At the end of this story, Jesus asked, "Which person showed kindness?"

T. J. raised his hand.

"T. J., do you know where we can get a coonskin cap for Jason?" asked Mrs. Meyer.

"I'll bring mine," he replied.

"Thank you, T. J.," said the teacher, checking it off her list. She never knew how hard it had been for T. J. to offer this kindness. But T. J. knew, and Jesus knew, too.

The big day finally came. The canoe carriers drew the biggest laughs when the canoe caught the tip of the flag. With quick action, they unwrapped the flag and rescued the canoe from tipping. Everyone clapped loudly as Jason stepped over the last painted mountain.

Judging by the audience's cheers, Jason had been a very successful leader. After the show, congratulations were shared all around, and props were returned.

"Thanks, T. J.," Jason said, handing him the ball of fur. "This was a great cap."

"You were the best Daniel Boone I ever saw," T. J. said honestly.

So always . . . be kind.
—Colossians 3:12 NCV

The True Test

A Story about Trust

"That's going to be a hard test tomorrow," Cole said with a worried look.

Kate nodded. It would be especially hard for her since she had misplaced her social studies book.

"Can I copy that list of words at the end of the chapter?" Kate asked. "I can probably remember the definitions."

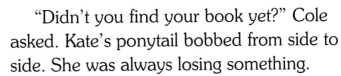

"Didn't you find your book yet?" Cole asked. Kate's ponytail bobbed from side to side. She was always losing something.

Kate hunched over the borrowed book. Scribbling the last few words, Kate slammed the book shut.

"Thanks," she said. "Maybe I can still find my book before tomorrow."

Cole settled down to study right after school. *How could Kate ever earn a passing grade without the textbook?* he wondered. Cole carefully reviewed everything, and by early evening he had finished studying.

"Cole," his mother called. "Kate is on the phone."

Kate sounded frantic. "Cole, can I borrow your social studies book? I can't remember half these definitions."

Cole considered Kate's request. She had already lost her book. If he trusted her, would she lose his book, too? Silence settled over the phone lines as he remembered a story he had heard about trust.

Jesus sat quietly on the shore as evening came. The scene beneath Him was bathed in the colors of a glorious sunset. After a busy day among crowds of people, Jesus was grateful for the calm. He could see His disciples as they rowed across the lake.

Jesus watched the men in the boat pulling the oars.

Night came. The wind whipped whitecaps on the lake. Clouds gathered. Darkness fell quickly as thickening clouds covered the moon. As the disciples reached the middle of the lake, strong waves lapped over the sides of the boat.

The men were tossed from side to side as the storm grew stronger. Frantically the disciples struggled to control their boat as the winds beat against them.

Jesus saw their problem, so He went to help them. Jesus was not bothered by the raging storm.

The disciples were terrified when they saw a figure walking toward them on the water! They didn't know it was Jesus.

"Don't be afraid," Jesus called calmly. "It is I."

But Peter wasn't sure. He said, "If it's really You, Lord, then let me come to You."

"Come," said Jesus.

Peter cautiously stepped over the side of the unsteady boat.

Peter walked on the water toward Jesus. But the storm hadn't stopped. Wind whipped Peter's robe, and the sounds of the angry waves filled his ears. Peter stopped trusting Jesus.

Peter started to sink.

The next morning, Cole had mixed feelings as he walked toward the playground. He liked helping a friend, but he hoped he had been right to trust Kate with his textbook.

"Look, Cole," Kate called, holding up a book. It was the class textbook, but the back cover flopped loosely as Kate came closer.

Cole's heart sank as he wondered, *How could Kate ruin my book in just one night?*

"I found my book," Kate said happily, tucking away her book with the floppy cover. "Here's yours. Thanks for the loaner."

"And," she added, "thanks for trusting me."

*The person who trusts
in the Lord will be blessed.*
—Jeremiah 17:7 NCV

Ball Hog

A Story about Humility

"Calm down, everybody," hushed the coach. "I know this is for the championship, but remember the basics: Keep your eye on the ball. Play your position. And pass the ball to your teammates."

"Don't just go for the goal," yelled Jason.

The team members smirked knowingly. All season, Jason had "hogged" the ball and grabbed the glory for each win.

A loud cheer came from the group as eleven yellow shirts raced back on the field. Saying a quick prayer, Kate asked Jesus to help her play well.

Screech! The referee's whistle signaled that the ball was in play. Yellow and green shirts tangled with arms and legs.

Amanda passed the ball to Kate. Kate controlled the ball. Closer, closer, she dribbled toward the goal.

Kate didn't have a clear shot to the goal. She needed to pass. She saw another yellow shirt—Jason, the ball hog himself! Make him the hero?

A green shirt slipped on the muddy ground. Jason had a clear, easy shot. She passed the ball to his yellow shirt.

Score! The whistle blew.

Yellow shirts crowded around Jason. "We won! We won!"

"Okay now, everybody," Coach called, trying to calm the crowd. "The photographer is waiting. Let's get the team together."

Jason elbowed his way to the front. He and Coach each held one side of the trophy. The photographer signaled Kate to the back edge of the group. Kate was thrilled that her team had won, but it seemed like only Jason was a winner.

I pass the winning ball and end up in the back row, she thought glumly.

Then, she remembered Jesus' story about a similar situation.

Jesus simply shook
His head. He had
been invited to dinner at the
home of a community leader. Guests
rudely elbowed their way to the best seats.
That's when Jesus told this story:
    Wedding music filled the air.
    Musicians blew flutes, strummed harps, and rattled
castanets as the guests gathered to watch the
procession of the bride and groom.

Caleb moved along in the background. Hidden by the laughing guests, he crept closer to the home where the feast would be held. *I will be first to reach the dining hall,* he thought. *Watching the procession is nice, but eating at the best table is far more important.*

Soon the wedding feast lay
before him. Only a servant moved among
the tables to add goblets. Caleb strode directly
to the front.

Studying the tables carefully, he finally said,
"Here, this is the best seat in the house."

Caleb chuckled and settled himself comfortably as the other guests scrambled to find seats, filling even the bad ones behind pillars at the back of the room. The musicians led the happy couple and their attendants to the front of the room.

Caleb sat back and watched.

"Excuse me." Caleb felt a tap on his shoulder. "This seat is reserved for one of the bridal attendants."

Caleb angrily stood up. "But I've been waiting here during the whole procession!"

"I'm sorry, sir," said the host. "There are still some seats left."

Caleb swirled his cloak and stomped away, searching for a seat. Finally, he slumped down next to a dripping fountain behind a stone ledge.

Jesus explained to those around Him, "Don't take a place of honor, because a more distinguished person may have been invited.

"Instead, take a less important place. Then, your host can move you up to a better place. All the guests then will see the way you are honored."

The photographer called for quiet. "I'll take the shot on the count of three," he said. "One . . ."

Coach glanced around proudly at his team. "Two . . ."

The coach caught Kate's eye.

"Wait a minute," said Coach, reaching out his hand. "Kate should be here. She gave up shots all season so the team would have a better chance to score. Why, she even passed the winning shot to Jason. Come on up here, Kate."

Teammates congratulated Kate as she made her way to the front of the group.

Coach reached out and put Kate's hands on the trophy. "We're proud of you, Kate," he whispered.

Jason looked across at Kate. He smiled. "Uh, thanks for the assist . . ."

"One, two, three!" the photographer counted quickly. Flash.

All who make themselves great will be made humble, but those who make themselves humble will be made great.
—Luke 14:11 NCV

The Good Things in Life

A Story about Thankfulness

"These are yummy," said Amanda, licking a melted chocolate chip off her hand. Kate's mom always had a special treat waiting for Kate and her friends on Friday afternoons.

"Thanks a lot, Mrs. Taylor," said Cole, taking an extra cookie as he dashed out the door ahead of his friends. He was eager to leave on a weekend camping trip.

"See ya!" he called.

Amanda and T. J. walked another block before T. J. admitted, "I'm so glad it's finally Friday."

Amanda smiled knowingly. Since his birthday on Tuesday, T. J. had talked eagerly about spending the entire weekend playing his new computer game.

T. J. turned at the next corner, and Amanda walked the last two blocks alone.

"Meow." Tiger rubbed Amanda's leg as she came through the door. The cat then jumped on the sofa, ready for a long cuddle. Amanda patted her lap, and Tiger immediately accepted the invitation.

Quiet settled around Amanda as she thought back to the walk home.

Kate's mom had baked fresh cookies. Cole was going camping. T. J. had a new computer game. Amanda compared her life with that of her friends. Blinking away a tear, she sighed deeply.

"I *should* feel thankful for what I have instead of being jealous of my friends," she told Tiger, but the word 'thankful' seemed hollow. As Tiger purred, Amanda remembered a story about thankfulness.

Jesus and His disciples almost missed
seeing the men. The small group huddled
together outside a village, away from
everyone else. After a brief glance at the
group, the disciples hurried along. They
knew the men were very sick. Bandages
covered large sores on their skin.

The sick men had to live away from their friends and families forever, unless the priests agreed that they were healed of the horrible disease.

As Jesus walked down the road, ten of the sick men called out to Him. With pitiful wails they begged, "Jesus, please heal us. Master, have mercy on us."

Jesus looked toward them. He saw the lonely, hurting men, so terribly scarred by the disease. He called back, "Go and show yourselves to the priests."

The men hurried toward town. If the priests said they were healed, the men could return to their families. They could work at jobs. They could take off their bandages. As the ten men ran to the priests, they realized their skin had returned to normal. The bumps and sores were gone. Jesus had healed them all!

While the other men ran on, one man stopped. He turned around and walked all the way back to Jesus. Even though the priests had not yet said the man was healed, he came close to Jesus and knelt in the dust at Jesus' feet.

"Thank You, Lord," he said. "Thank You."

Jesus asked, "Didn't I heal ten of you? Are the others too busy to thank Me?"

Jesus then said to the man, "You may get up and go to the priests. I'm glad you came back to say 'thank you.'"

"Amanda?" her dad called.

"We're here," Amanda said
as Tiger stood up, only to settle
back down on Amanda's lap.

"Are we saving money on electricity?" her dad joked. "I didn't
see any lights."

"I can think better in the dark," said Amanda with a smile.

"Want to share your thoughts?" her dad asked.

"I was thinking about the good things in my life," Amanda said. "I have great friends. We have a nice house, and we had a super soccer team this year."

Her dad nodded and then gently tapped her forehead.

"Anything else up there you want to share?" he asked, moving to sit beside her.

"Yeow!" yelped Tiger, as Amanda's dad sat too close for cat comfort. Puffing out her tail, Tiger stalked away.

"My cat loves me most of the time," smiled Amanda. "And you and Jesus always love me."

The two sat quietly as evening shadows lengthened. "Yes," her dad whispered softly, "Jesus gives us a lot to be thankful for."

We always thank God for . . . you.
—1 Thessalonians 1:2 NCV

Looking to the Bible

You can read more about Jesus and the Bible characters
in this book by looking at these stories.

The Miraculous Catch of Fish
From *A Story about Obedience*   John 21:2–14

Through the Roof
From *A Story about Friendship*   Luke 5:17–25

The Son Who Left Home
From *A Story about Forgiveness*   Luke 15:11–24

Zacchaeus the Tax Collector
From *A Story about Honesty*   Luke 19:1–10

The Good Samaritan
From *A Story about Kindness*   Luke 10:25–37

Peter Walks on Water
From *A Story about Trust*   Matthew 14:22–33

A Place of Honor
From *A Story about Humility*   Luke 14:7–11

The Ten Lepers
From *A Story about Thankfulness*   Luke 17:11–19